LIVING IN
CHINA

Written and Illustrated by
REGAN SHEDDAN

Published in the United States of America

ISBN: 978-1-7369141-0-6

珠
海

Gongbei Port is the border crossing station between China and Macau. It is always crowded with people walking across. People go to Macau to gamble, and they go to China to buy fresh vegetables.

珠海

The Fisher Girl statue comes from a Chinese legend about a dragon girl who disguised herself as a human in order to live in Zhuhai. She found a huge pearl in the sea, representing the beauty of the city.

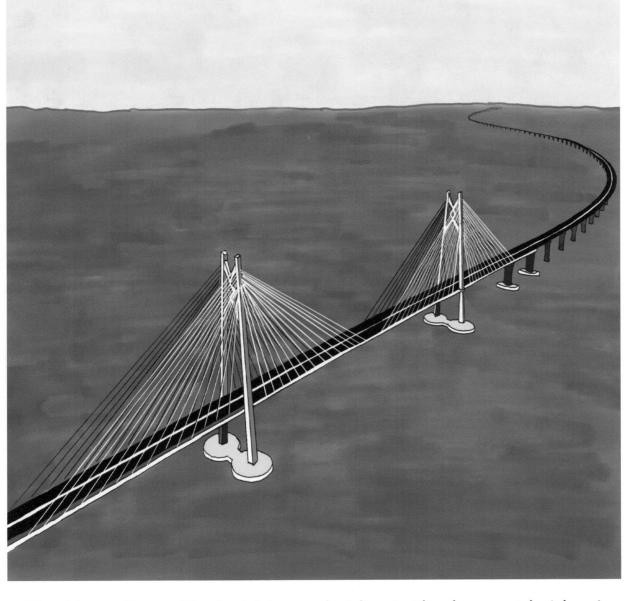

珠海

The Hong Kong-Zhuhai-Macau bridge is the longest bridge in the world. It connects three countries, and it only takes twenty minutes to cross. In a few places, the bridge goes under water.

珠海

While driving along Lover's Road, it is hard to miss the lighthouse. Used only for decoration, it is a popular place to take wedding photos. At night, people gather to dance and exercise to music.

珠
海

The Zhuhai Opera House is shaped like seashells and is built on a man-made island. Inside the shells, people from all over the world come to perform on the big stage in ballets, musicals, and plays.

珠海

The beach is always crowded with people playing in the sand, walking in the water, and flying kites. However, people do not go out until after four o'clock because they don't want to get a tan.

珠海

Chimelong Ocean Kingdom is the largest aquarium in the world with five world records. People love seeing the beluga whale show, taking pictures with dolphins, and riding water roller coasters.

珠
海

Haibin Park is across the street from the beach, and it is fun to take relaxing walks and fly kites. There are millions of flowers, and new ones are planted every two weeks to keep them fresh and beautiful.

珠海

The seafood market is made up of stalls lining the streets. People can buy seafood to take home, or they can pick their favorites and have a nearby restaurant cook the fresh food for only two dollars!

珠海

Huafa Mall is the biggest mall in Zhuhai, China. It is a western-style mall with a clear roof. The walls are open, so people can feel the fresh air while they are shopping. The mall even has a Starbucks!

广州

Canton Tower is a cool building in Guangzhou and the tallest
TV tower in Asia. China loves light shows, so they often light up
the buildings with colorful lights and shine lasers in the sky.

The Symphony Ferris Wheel in Zhongshan is a new way to see the city from up high. In order to see the city easily from different angles, the wheel takes twenty minutes to go around one time.

广东

Every Chinese New Year, cities across Guangdong province open local flower markets. At these markets, hundreds of people set up tents to sell their beautiful flowers. Don't forget to bargain for a low price!

中山

1866—1925

Sun Wen Memorial Park is located near the city center of Zhongshan. Both the park and the city are named after the same man, Sun Zhongshan. He is known as the father of modern China.

In addition to flower markets, many cities have parades to celebrate Chinese New Year. Dragon dances are popular, and thousands of people cheer as they parade down the streets.

东莞

While the buildings in this city may look like apartments, they are factories. In Dongguan, workers from across China come to work in the factories here, and the skies are often clouded with pollution.

东莞

The most famous park in Dongguan is Keyuan. The water is bright green with algae, and fish swim in the ponds. Children feed the fish, while their parents appreciate the traditional architecture of China.

北京

The Forbidden City is the biggest ancient palace in the world and contains almost nine thousand rooms. It is surrounded by a tall wall, and only the imperial family and the servants were allowed inside.

北京

The Temple of Heaven was built so emperors could worship the God of Heaven. The temple complex is four times larger than the Forbidden City to show that God is greater than man.

北京

The Great Wall of China was built hundreds of years ago to protect China from enemy attacks. It is the same length as half of the equator, and more than one million people died working to build it.

北京

The Summer Palace is a beautiful garden of lakes, temples, pavilions, bridges, and flowers that was built for the emperor's family. One of the empresses used it as her summer resort.

广州

Chimelong Safari Park in Guangzhou is full of animals, and it has the largest white tiger exhibit in the world. The park's main attraction is the panda triplets, which are the only surviving set in the world.

阳
朔

Yangshuo's scenery can be seen on the twenty-yuan bill.
People love traveling down the river on bamboo rafts past the
unique mountains and exploring the colorful caves in the area.

昆明

When exploring Nanping Business Walking Street, you will surely encounter cultural artwork and sculptures unique to Kunming. A snack center offers pedestrians a taste of local food as well.

张家界

Zhangjiajie National Park has inspired Chinese art for a long time. It has the world's longest glass bridge, longest cable car ride, and tallest outdoor elevator, which is also made of glass.

哈尔滨

Harbin Ice and Snow World is famous for having ice castles and ice sculptures for more than one month every year. At night, lights from inside the castles make the ice sparkle in different colors.

哈尔滨

The Chinese city of Harbin has been heavily influenced by Russia. Saint Sophia Cathedral is the largest Eastern Orthodox Church in far east Asia, and it is now a large, cultural art gallery.

湖南

Many Chinese people live in small homes in the mountains, and they work in the fields all day long. They build rice terraces to make sure the rice and vegetables always have enough water to grow.

西安

The Terracotta Warriors were buried with a Chinese emperor. Over 8,000 warriors, 130 chariots, and 670 horses have been dug up with many more still buried. No two statues are alike!

西安

In ancient China, the bell tower in Xi'an rang every morning to announce the new day. Directly across from it, in the drum tower, drums were beat every night to mark the end of the day.

西安

Muslim Quarter in Xi'an is home to 60,000 Muslims and is famous for its food. All the dishes such as noodles, soup, bread, and candy are handmade, and the aroma of spices is hard to resist.

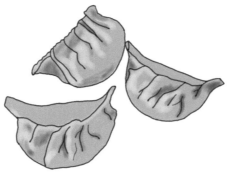

Dumplings are sheets of dough carefully folded around a delicious filling.

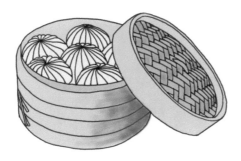

Dim-Sum is traditional Cantonese food steamed in bamboo baskets.

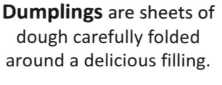

Lanzhou Beef Noodles is the most popular Muslim dish in China.

Rice is eaten with every meal.

Mooncakes are given at Mid Autumn Festival, and they are filled with red beans or egg yolks.

Eggs and Tomato is a common dish.

ABOUT THE AUTHOR

Regan Sheddan was born in Tennessee and moved to China as a young child. She spent ten years growing up, surrounded by Chinese culture. Regan always wanted to read children's books about her home, but the only ones she could find were about tourist locations. The pictures in her book are self-illustrated and from her personal experiences. Aside from writing and drawing, Regan is a third-degree black belt in Taekwondo and loves to sing, bake, and play with her dogs.

"China is more than a big country. It has a unique culture with the most amazing people. To me, it is home, and I want others to see the China that I know and love."

- Regan Sheddan

CPSIA information can be obtained
at www.ICGtesting.com
Printed in the USA
BVHW020039080521
606754BV00002B/14